SPHRAGISTI

The study of seals is called sphragistics. Most of
greatly enlarged from seals, either from the actual dies which were
down on wax or paper, or from the impressions on the wax or paper, or from
seals on various printings. When a government or reign changed, a new seal was
often brought into use, and the old die would generally be destroyed. This
was intended to prevent forgeries, for seals were meant to confirm and
authenticate very important documents. Wax seals are fragile and often break,
and they easily fall off of documents, or rub away or melt. There are not now
many left to us from early seventeenth-century America.

Most of the American colonies at first belonged to proprietors, who made
their own laws and grants of land. Some proprietors used their own family arms
as seals. Others used proud American natives, or items of commerce, such as
beaver, trees, fish, or agricultural products. In time, royal government took
over from the proprietors, and the proprietors' seals were replaced by seals with
the monarch on one side, the Royal Arms on the other. The monarch would
be shown receiving offerings of the colony's wealth from an American native
on bended knee (the colonies lost many privileges when transferred to royal
control). Pelts, tobacco and silk were offered. Americans, and certainly last of
all native Americans, never truly kneeled well to anyone; these royal seals
(excepting the earliest, Virginia's, shown here) have not been used in this book
because they are rather similar to each other, and the emblems that follow are
meant to be the American colonies' own. Consequently we show seals either
from the early, dark ages of our colonial history, or from the end of it, like
the sword-in-hand seal on the cover.

Virginia, 1606

Virginia, 1606

When British troops marched into Boston in 1768, the Province's seal disappeared. Three sessions of the Provincial Congress passed without a seal. On
July 19, 1775, a committee was appointed in the House to provide a seal, and
they recommended that the device of the old Provincial seal, with the Royal
Arms, should not be used. Instead they suggested a seal similar to the one on
their first charter, but in place of an Indian with tomahawk and liberty cap,
there should be an English American, holding a sword in his right hand and
Magna Carta in his left. The motto *Ense Petit Placidam sub Libertate Quietam*
would be written around it. This was taken from a line by Algernon Sydney:
Manus haec inimica tryannis ense petit placidam sub libertate quietam (This
hand, an enemy of tyrants, by the sword seeks peace and quiet under liberty).
Sydney's *Discourses Concerning Government* were first published in 1698 and
new editions came out in 1763 and 1772. The line refers to his principle that
all government should of right be based on the consent of the governed. These
arms and motto were accepted on August 7, 1775. A few days later bills of
credit were authorized, to be engraved by Paul Revere. Each note bore a similar figure with the words "Issued in defence of American liberty."

From the flag of the
Bedford Minutemen,
1775

THE VIRGINIA COMPANY

Expeditions to America went out in 1578 and in 1583 under Sir Humphrey Gilbert, who was lost at sea in the second as he is said to have said: "we are as near to heaven by sea as by land." Sir Richard Grenville was sent out in 1584 by his cousin Walter Raleigh, Esquire (who was knighted later, upon the return of this expedition), half-brother of Sir H. Gilbert, and "that part of the country now called Virginia" was discovered and taken possession of in the name of Queen Elizabeth I. Grenville landed in Florida and soon went up to an island they called Roanoke. In 1586 Grenville led another expedition to Roanoke with seven ships and a hundred men sent out by Sir Walter Raleigh. These people had to be rescued by Sir Francis Drake, who happened to be in the neighborhood. Grenville had gone to England for supplies, but was back at Roanoke just after Drake had left. Fifteen men remained from Grenville's ships, but only their bones were found by the next expedition. In 1587 Raleigh and Grenville sent out 150 people —17 of them women — to settle in Virginia. They landed in what is now North Carolina and then went to Roanoke. On August 18 of that year, Virginia Dare was born there, the first English child born in America and named after her birth place.

In 1606 two competing companies obtained patents from King James I for the settlement of Virginia: the London Company — the adventurers (or investors) were from London, to occupy regions between 34° and 38°, and the Plymouth Company — adventurers from that town, between 41° and 45° of latitude; either company could settle the land between. The London adventurers, or, as they were called, the Virginia Company of London, sent out three ships under Captain Newport, and with him went dauntless John Smith, to found a colony at Jamestown. The Plymouth Company's expedition that year for the "North Plantation of Virginia" was taken at sea by the Spanish. The Plymouth Company then sent an expedition to Maine in the following year, but it returned home in 1608 as "North Virginia was not habitable for Englishmen." And as to the southern settlement, we all know the story of Captain Smith, Powhattan and Pocahontas.

A ship for Virginia, from *Nova Britannia, Offering Most Excellent fruites by Planting in Virginia,* 1609

Here are the arms of the Virginia Company, which were granted in 1610 and became the arms of the colony. The shield bears the red cross of Saint George and the arms of England and France quartered with Scotland and Ireland. A crowned Virginia (Queen Elizabeth I) is on the crest. The armed supporters have Saint George's cross on their breast plates. The motto means: *Virginia gives a fifth crown.* The poet Spencer, Raleigh's friend, had dedicated the *Fairie Queene* in 1596 to "Elizabeth . . . By the Grace of God Queene of England, Fraunce and Ireland, and of Virginia." Scotland, the fourth kingdom was added in 1603.

From *The Generall Historie of Virginia, New-England and the Summer Isles* by Captain John Smith, 1624

VIRGINIA

EN DAT QUINTVM

PLYMOUTH

King James I called the Puritans "a sect insufferable" and swore he would "harry them out of the kingdom." Some went to Amsterdam and then to Leyden, "a fair and beautiful city." They were "Pilgrims," and they hoped to advance the gospel in remote parts of the world — the New World. The ships *Speedwell* and *Mayflower* were chartered, and on July 22, 1620, the Pilgrims sailed from Delfthaven on the *Speedwell* to Southampton, where the *Mayflower* awaited them. Two weeks later both ships sailed westward; the *Speedwell* sprang a leak, and both ships returned. The *Mayflower* left once more on September 6, with 100 passengers. On November 9, the coast of Cape Cod was seen, and the *Mayflower* came to anchor at what later became Provincetown. Here a "Compact" was drawn up "to combine themselves and to frame just and equal laws." On December 11, 1620, the Pilgrims landed at Plymouth Rock, and on the 20th they began to build dwellings out of logs and thatch. It was a deathly cold winter, and 44 of the Pilgrims died.

In the spring of 1621, the Pilgrims met Massasoit, chief of the Wampanoags, and a peace treaty was made. The chief later became ill, and one of the Pilgrims, Edward Winslow, saved Massasoit's life with herbs and medicines. In November, nearly a year after their arrival, and after a good harvest from twenty-six acres that had been planted, Massasoit and his tribesmen were invited to a Thanksgiving feast with the Pilgrims.

One year after their arrival the *Fortune* appeared, bringing 35 souls and a new patent from the Council for New England, "better than the former, with less limitation." Then other ships arrived, bringing nearly 60 men who settled at Wessagusset, the first plantation in Boston Harbor. These settlers stirred up the Indians there, and though saved by Miles Standish, some, frightened, returned to England, and others went to New Plymouth.

The settlers at Plymouth often found themselves in want, one reason being droughts and another a clause in their compact "by which all that was raised in the colony was placed in common stock." Rain came, clothes and cattle were brought from England by Edward Winslow, and the laws of the colony were changed.

On the title page of the Plymouth Records is an illustration of the colony's seal, and there is a die of it belonging to the Pilgrim Society at Plymouth. The shield is divided by a red cross of Saint George, and on either side of the kneeling Indian in each quarter is a small pine tree.

Plymouth

NEW NETHERLAND

Henry Hudson on *The Half Moon (de Halve Maen)*, sailed by Manhattan Island in 1609. In 1613 Captains Adrian Block in the *Tiger* and Hendrick Christensen in the *Fortune* arrived there and soon Dutchmen were trading for furs with the natives. The *Tiger* burned up shortly after their arrival, and the yacht *Restless (Onrust)* was built using parts salvaged from the remains. Captain Block with maps and charts went back to Amsterdam the next year, and the *Restless* was left in charge of Cornelis Hendricksen. Hendricksen took more charts home two years later, together with intriguing reports of the place. In 1621 the Chartered West India Company *(Geoctroyerde Westindische Compagnie* in Dutch) was established, and in 1623 merchants of Amsterdam began making arrangements to colonize New Netherland with Captain Cornelis May as Director. The seal from which the plate opposite was taken was in use from that year until 1664.

The beaver, on a silver shield, represented *in bend* or diagonally, was then the chief commodity of New Netherland. In 1626, 7,246 beaver skins were sent to Amsterdam, and by 1671, 80,000 skins a year were sent. The beaver was surrounded by a string of wampum, which represented wealth. The coronet crest symbolized that the province was invested with the arms of a count by their Highmightynesses, the States General.

Seal of the Dutch West India Company *(Geoctroyerde Westindische Compagnie)* enlarged from ½" in width; New York Secretary of State, Albany.

New Netherland, 1623

NEW AMSTERDAM

In 1625 Willem Verhulst took over as Director, and began to establish a permanent settlement on Manhattan Island. The next year Peter Minuit was in charge, and bought Manhattan for 60 guilders ($24.00, it has always been said) worth of merchandise. Fort *Nieu Amsterdam* was built on the southern end of the island, and buildings soon grew up around it. The new little town was also called *Nieu Amsterdam.* The town's first seal was sent there on the ship *Peartree* in 1654, to Peter Stuyvesant, the sixth governor of New Netherland. It had a silver shield and the arms on it dated from 1342, when the people of old Amsterdam were freed by the Count of Holland from bearing various heavy economic crosses. There were therefore three white crosses on a black stripe (pale) in the center, and the other stripes were red. Above was the draped flag of their national hero, the Prince of Orange, which had wide horizontal stripes of orange, white and blue. The monogram GWC of the Company is in the cartouche above the crest, a beaver.

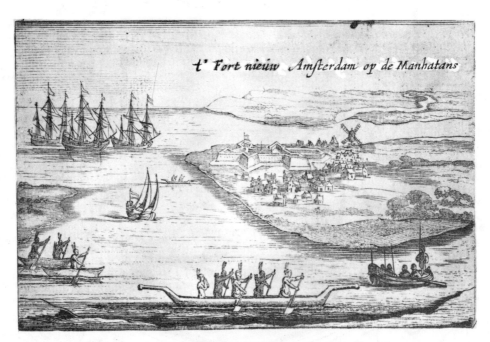

The earliest view of

New Amsterdam, from *Beschrijvinghe van Virginia, Nieuw Nederlandt, Nieuw Engelandt,* 1651

. . . this sun of York

Take it, brave York . . .

In 1664, when the Dutch surrendered to the English, the inhabitants were ordered "not to call this place otherwise than New York, on the Island of Manhattans, in America." King Charles II that year granted the province to his brother, the duke of York, from whom the city now took its name; about this, more follows. A badge of the dukes of York, was a rising sun, which you know from Shakespeare's *King Richard III.* A rising sun was used on colonial bills of New York and on the first seal of the State of New York in 1777.

SIGILLVM·AMSTELLO DAMENSIS·IN·NOVO·BELGIO

New Amsterdam

THE COUNCIL FOR NEW ENGLAND

The Adventurers of the Northern Colony of Virginia received a patent in 1620 assigning them the territory between 40° and 48° which had been under the control of the Virginia Company. They were then known as The Council for New England. The Pilgrim Fathers had tried in 1617 to obtain permission from the Virginia Company to settle within this territory, but did not succeed because of their religious beliefs. In 1620 a grant was made by the Virginia Company to John Pierce, and it was under his patent that the Pilgrims sailed. By the time they arrived in Massachusetts, though, the territory had been separated and the patent was no longer considered good. Pierce then applied for a new patent. This was received in 1621, and stated that if the land chosen was surveyed within seven years, a patent would be given for the territory. Pierce and the Pilgrims soon had a falling out; to settle the differences the Council for New England gave the Pilgrims the land they occupied, and Pierce was given the rest. This quarrel was important in the setting up of another colony in Massachusetts, for some of the Plymouth Adventurers became associated with the Bay Company, as follows.

Puritans had settled at Cape Ann in 1623, forming what is known as the Dorchester Company. That failed in 1626, and everything was transferred to Salem. The Council for New England then made a grant, now lost, and The New England Company for a Plantation in Massachusetts Bay came into being in 1628, made up largely of Puritan adventurers. Now the president of the Council for New England was the earl of Warwick, and he was one of the grantees of a parcel of land on Massachusetts Bay, 10 miles by 30 at the bottom of the Bay. Robert Gorges was made governor of that territory. The earl began making grants, it seems, and he and the Council soon had a falling out about this. The Council's seal, then in the earl's keeping, was asked for. The seal was promised, but not sent. It was asked for again and again. It seems as though Captain Gorges enlarged upon the grant and seized a good amount of territory, and rode over the heads of the Council. The Council's grants disappeared, and so did the seals attached with them. The Patent of New Plymouth, 1629, has the seal, but it is defaced. The arms opposite are from the title pages of Captain John Smith's *Generall Historie,* with an abridged map of Virginia and New England. "Near the part representing Virginia are placed, the arms of Virginia [seen elsewhere here]; and near the coast of New England are placed the arms, which I now venture to call the arms of the Council for New England," wrote a scholar over a century ago. The motto, *Gens incognita mihi serviet* is no doubt from Psalm 18, 43: "A people whom I have not known shall serve me." The lower compartment of the shield is "barry wavy of six, argent and azure," that is, waves of blue and silver. The Royal Arms of England, quartered with the Harp of Erin and Lion of Scotland are in the upper compartment. The crest is Neptune on a sea-horse, and the female supporters represent wisdom and science.

COGNITA MIHI

GENS IN

SERVIET

The Council for New-England

THE GOVERNOR AND COMPANY OF THE
MASSACHUSETTS BAY

IN NEW ENGLAND, 1629

The settlement of the Dorchester Company at Cape Ann having ended in 1626, Roger Conant moved with his followers to Naumkeag, which was later to be called Salem. Mr. Conant was promised that if he and the settlers would stay there, a patent would be obtained which would grant them "that part of New England lying between three miles to the north of the Merrimack and three miles to the south of the Charles River, and of every part thereof, in the Massachusetts Bay; and in length between the described breadth, from the Atlantic Ocean to the South Sea." The patent was obtained in 1628. A partnership was formed with several London merchants, and the Massachusetts Company soon resulted to carry on the plantation of the Dorchester men. John Endicott, a leading man of the Company, left England in 1628 with a few emigrants, and arrived later that year at Naumkeag where he began his duties as governor. By the end of 1629, there were about 100 people in the colony. The next year new arrivals came, and a local government was set up to be called "The Governor and Company of London's Plantation in the Massachusetts Bay, in New England," with Endicott as governor, subordinate to the company in England. In April 1629, the Company wrote Governor Endicott that they had sent by Mr. Samuel Sharpe, a passenger on the *George*, the Company's seal, made of silver. An Indian with flowing hair and a girdle of leaves was on it; the newcomers of course were already mindful of their neighbors, and had adopted a just and honorable policy towards the Indians — territory was only to be bought and not taken by force. The seal also had a cross, and a ribbon coming from the mouth of the Indian with the words "Come over and help us," and little pine trees behind. The seal, or a later copy of it, was in use until 1684, when the colonial charter was terminated. Then it was succeeded by the Royal Arms, which were in use until 1784.

Seal of the Governor and Society of the Massachusetts Bay in New-England

NEW HAMPSHIRE

Captain John Smith first discovered the Pascatagua River, and there he found a safe harbor. In 1606 King James' patent of Virginia divided the territory into North and South Virginia; South Virginia was granted to adventurers of London, and North Virginia to adventurers of Bristol, Plymouth and Exeter. The latter became "The council established at Plymouth in the county of Devon for the planting, ruling and governing of New-England in America." Their territories extended from 40° to 48° of northern latitude. "Their patent, or charter, was the foundation of all the grants that were made of the country of New-England."

Captain Weymouth had been searching for a northwest passage when he put in at Pemaquid. From there he returned to old Plymouth with five natives. Sir Fernando Gorges, the captain of the fort at Plymouth, was also a member of the council. He took the Indians into his service and from them learned much about their country.

Captain John Mason had been a London merchant, a sea captain, governor of Newfoundland, and then governor of Portsmouth in Hampshire. In 1621 he received from the council a grant of the territory from Naumkeag (now Salem) to the Merrimack, and all the way up to the beginning of those rivers, the territory being called *Mariana*. In 1622 Sir Fernando Gorges and Captain Mason received a grant together of the lands between the Merrimack and the Sagadehock (Kennebec) rivers. This was called *Laconia* (the name of ancient Sparta). Gorges and Mason, with other adventurers, became the Company of Laconia in 1623 to establish a colony and fishery on the Pascatagua River. That year the first settlements were made at Portsmouth (Strawberry Bank) and Dover (Hilton's Point).

In 1629 settlers from Massachusetts bought land in the neighborhood of Pascatagua from chiefs Passaconaway, Runnaawitt, Wahongnonawit and Rowls. During this year Captain Mason received a new patent from the council at Plymouth for the land from the middle of the river to its beginning, then northwestward; and through the Merrimack river to its beginning, and then westward. This was to be called NEW HAMPSHIRE. Gorges received the territory east of the Pascatagua River, Maine. Other patents were made, and these sometimes conflicted with each other.

The people of New Hampshire soon found problems with the different proprietary claims, and, unable to do anything about it themselves, they decided in 1641 to be governed by Massachusetts. This situation continued until 1679, when it was determined in England that the Massachusetts authority over New Hampshire was unlawful. Then New Hampshire became a separate province.

This is the last seal of the Colony of New Hampshire, the first colony to adopt a constitution. The old royal seal was discarded, and this seal (the original was 1¾ inch in diameter) took its place in 1775. The motto means *Strength united is stronger.* The fish and the tree represented the colony's industries, and the five bound arrows represented the colony's five counties.

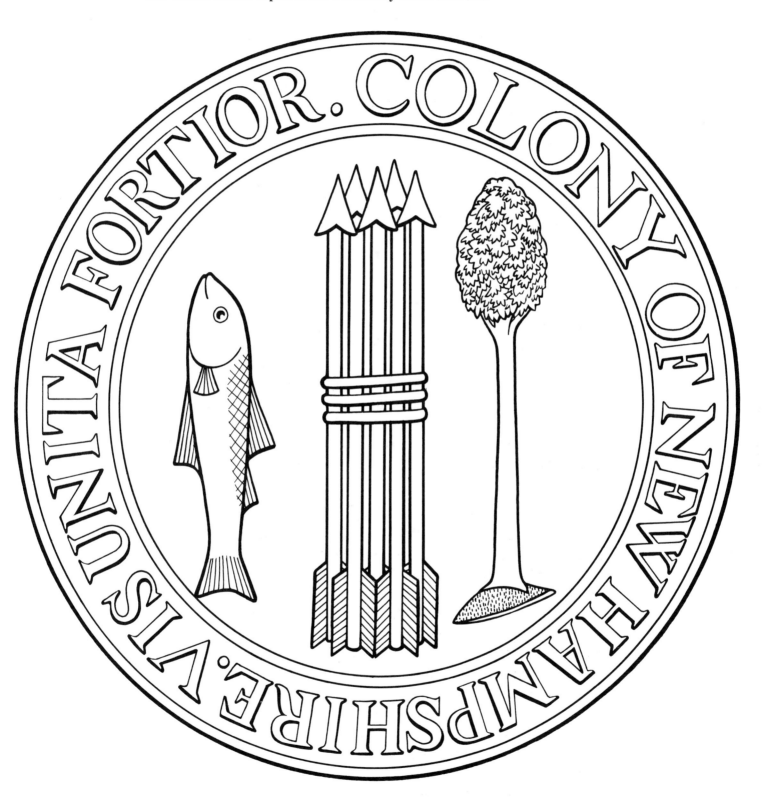

From the actual die preserved in the New England Historic-Genealogical Society, Boston

MARYLAND

George Calvert was born in 1582 and baptized in the Church of England. Thirteen years later he went to Oxford, and in 1606 he received an appointment to look after records in Ireland. In 1609 he was a member of the Virginia Company. In time, he went to work as a secretary to the great Cecil, secretary of state, and soon lord high treasurer to the king. Calvert was knighted in 1617, and soon he himself became secretary of state. He also was to represent Oxford University in Parliament. When the king gave him lands in Ireland, he moved there. In 1620 he bought a large part of Newfoundland, and he sent some colonists there to a settlement he called Avalon.

In 1624 Sir George became a Catholic, and the next year he became an Irish peer — baron of Baltimore. The king was fond of him in spite of his conversion — Catholics were not then popular in England. But Lord Baltimore gave up his seat on the Privy Council and went to settle his new colony where he found only "eight or nine months of winter and nothing but rocks." So in 1629 he went to Virginia with his wife and some of his ten children, to look for a better place for his colonists. But when he arrived there, Lord Baltimore refused to take the oath of supremacy, for he believed the pope to be the head of the church, not the king. The Virginians therefore would not let him settle there. So Lord Baltimore thought about the unsettled territory around the Chesapeake Bay. He left his wife and children in Virginia and sailed for England to obtain a grant for his own territory. This he received; he could "have any part not already granted" and he would contribute his best endeavors to enlarge his majesty's Empire in that part of the world. The king would not allow Lord Baltimore to return to America, though, for he liked having him in England. So he sent for Lady Baltimore

No impressions exist of the first Great Seal; this is from a silver die, 3¾ inches in diameter, c. 1648. Annapolis

Maryland

and the children. Alas! On the way to England, the ship on which they had embarked sank.

In 1631 Lord Baltimore obtained a grant of that territory "lying to the southward of James River in Virginia, between that river and the bounds of Carolina," even though the governor of Virginia tried to stop the grant. Before he signed the charter, King Charles asked Lord Baltimore what he should call the territory, "who replied that he desired to have it called something in honor of his majesty's name, but that he was deprived of that happiness, there being already a province in those parts called Carolina. 'Let us therefore,' says the king, 'give it a name in honor of the Queen; what think you of *Mariana*?' To this his lordship expressed his dissent, it being the name of a Jesuit, who had written against monarchy. Whereupon the King proposed *Terra Mariae*, in English, Maryland, which was concluded on and inserted in the bill. And thus the proposed colony was named in honor of Henrietta Maria, daughter of Henry IV, king of France and Navarre, and sister of Louis XIII." Since the old Virginia Company objected, the attorney general advised Lord Baltimore to delay having the Charter put under the Great Seal "for some time." Before that came to pass, Lord Baltimore died on April 15, 1632, and was buried in Saint Dunstan's, Fleet Street, London.

Cecil Calvert succeeded his father and became Second Lord Baltimore, and Lord Proprietary of Maryland when he received the charter to Maryland. By this he could make grants of land and call assemblies and make laws, and he was, in his own province, "little less than a king." Leonard and George Calvert, Cecil's younger brothers, went to Maryland to establish the colony. The object was to provide a haven for persecuted Catholics. The good ship *Ark* and the small pinnace *Dove* took the two brothers "with very near twenty other gentlemen of very good fashion, and 300 laboring men well provided in all things." The settlers, by Lord Baltimore's charter, received the right to trade with Holland and elsewhere, which the Virginians could not do. Maryland could always undersell Virginia abroad with tobacco. The early Calverts' rule was mild and just, and "the heavy hand of royal government was unfelt." The liberties of the charter made the Marylanders feel as true freemen.

The Great Seal of Maryland was then and is now the family arms of the Lords Baltimore. All grants of land in the name of the Lord Proprietary were authenticated by the Great Seal of the Province. A seal of 1648 replaced one stolen in 1644 during the Ingle rebellion, and a third seal was used in 1657 and was still used in 1765. Here is the reverse side of Lord Baltimore's seal with the hereditary coat-of-arms. The first and forth quarters represented the Calvert family's arms, granted in 1622; they are, in heraldic language, paly of six pieces or (gold) and sable (black), a bend counter-charged. These represent palisades, a stockade or fortification, appropriate to one who had fortified a town; the diagonal band, or bend, represented, probably, a scaling

Maryland

ladder. The 2nd and 3rd quarters show the arms of the Crossland family, inherited by Cecil from his grandmother. In heraldic language this coat is quarterly, argent (silver) and gules (red) a cross bottony countercharged. The cross relates to the family name, as well as being a symbol of a Christian warrior. A quarterly field represented a shield broken in battle, and that the bearer had proved himself valiant. Above the shield is an earl's coronet, which was borne by the Lords Baltimore only in relation to their American province, which by the Charter had the rank of a County Palatine. The coronet is surmounted by a mount and cross, emblems of sovereign authority. Above is a steel helmet full-face, which indicates exercise of government by an absolute jurisdiction. In England he could only wear a baron's coronet and the helmet in profile, indicating feudal allegiance.

Above is the Calvert crest: two pennons attached to spears with the Calvert colors: dexter or (gold) the other sable (black), staves gules (red) issuing from a ducal coronet. The supporters are a plowman with a shover and a fisherman with a fish, representing colonists. Leopards, with the Calvert colors, were the proper supporters of Lord Baltimore's family arms. The Calvert motto, *Fatti maschi parole femine*, an ancient Italian proverb meaning "Manly Deeds, Womanly Words" or "Courage and Courtesy" if you like. Behind the shield and supporters is an ermine-lined mantle. Around the seal are the words *Scuto bonae voluntatis tuae coronasti nos*, from the Fifth Psalm, "with favor will thou compass him as with a shield." These are the historic arms of Maryland.

THE COLONY OF RHODE ISLAND
AND PROVIDENCE PLANTATIONS

Providence was settled first by the Rev. Wm. Blackstone in 1634 and by the Arnolds and then by Roger Williams in 1636. Providence and the town of Warwick together were called the Providence Plantations. Portsmouth was settled by Dr. Clarke in 1638 and Newport in 1639. They united together in 1640 and formed the Colony of Rhode Island. Roger Williams provided the name, Providence Plantations In The Narragansett Bay In New England. In 1663 the title became The Colony of Rhode Island & Providence Plantations. Here's how their settling was described in 1874 by Charles Miller:

> *Did you ever hear the story told,*
> *Of Roger Williams, the preacher bold,*
> *That settled this State in the days of old,*
> *This little State of Rhode Island.*

History is a misty fuzz, and repeats herself as the echo does;
What I don't guess at, somebody does, to settle the State of Rhode Island.

Our Hope Is In Thee O Lord, from a Colony Bill, Providence, 1750

Rhode Island

In sixteen hundred thirty-six,
Roger Williams got into a fix
By saucing the Governor of Massachusetts,
And skedaddled away to Rhode Island.

He crossed as everybody knew,
Skeekonk River in a birch canoe;
Just to save the tolls that were due
On the bridges above and below him.

Mr. Williams, it seemed, "hath broached & dyvulged dyvers new & dangerous opinions, against the aucthoritie of Magistrates, as also writt lies of Defamacon, both of the Magistrates & Churches here . . ." He had allowed, for instance, that the Natives were the true owners of the land, and that the civil magistrate's power extended only to the bodies and goods, and outward state of men, etc. Governor Winthrop suggested that he therefore go and preach to the Narragansett Indians, and there he went, with Providence as his guide. He first stayed with Chief Massasoit and learned his language, for he "desired not to be troubled with English company."

Dr. John Clarke visited Mr. Williams in 1638 at his new home. Intolerent Boston was banishing more souls, and Dr. Clarke was out looking for a home for them. Mr. Coddington came along and bought "the great island of Acquednecke" from chiefs Cannonicus and Miantunomii of the Narragansetts. A document known as the Portsmouth Compact was drawn up and signed by Coddington, Clarke and twenty-one others, and they did "in the presence of Jehovah incorporate ourselves into a Bodie Politick . . ."

In 1647 the four towns, now united, held a General Assembly at Portsmouth, and it was decided that "the Seale of the Province shall be an Anchor." A sketch of it was added, and here is a copy of it:

An ivory seal was used from the next year to 1660, and this had a similar anchor on a shield. In 1660 John Clarke had a new seal made in England, but no impression of it exists. In 1663 the name of the Colony was changed, and another seal was adopted the following year. This had around it the words Rhod Iland and providence plantations, "with the word Hope over the head of the Anker."

That anchor was fouled — it had a cable twisted around it. The association of an anchor with Hope is biblical, from Hebrews VI, 19. The emblem shown here is from a Rhode Island colony bill of 1750. The foul anchor remained on Rhode Island seals, with the exception of Governor Andros's seal which had the Royal Arms and effigy, from 1687-90, until 1875, when the original plain, un-fouled, was again adoped. The anchor, with the present color scheme, would be gold against a white shield surrounded by a blue belt.

From a sketch for a new seal made in 1865; Rhode Island Historical Society

"It is ordered, that a Manuel (hand) Seal shall be provided for the State (this
is the first use of this word in the Rhode Island archives) and that the Signet
or Engraving thereof, shall be a sheafe of Arrows bound up, and in the Liess
(leash) or Bond, this motto indented: *Amor vincet omnia* (Love conquers all)."
This decree was made in 1641 at Newport; no trace of this seal exists, so we
show instead a more recent use of Rhode Island's emblem of the bound arrows.

HARVARD COLLEGE

"After God had carried us safe to New England, and we had builded our houses, provided necessaries for our livelihood, reared convenient places for God's worship, and settled the civill government, one of the next things we longed for and looked after was to advance learning and perpetuate it to posterity; dreading to leave an illiterate ministry to the churches when our present ministers shall lie in the dust. And as we were thinking and consulting how to effect this great work, it pleased God to stir up the heart of one Mr. Harvard (a godly gentleman and a lover of learning, then living amongst us) to give the one half of his estate (it being in all about 1700*l*.) towards the erecting of a colledge and all his library. After him another gave 300*l*.; others after them cast in more, and the publique hand of the state added the rest. The colledge was by common consent appointed to be at Cambridge (a place very pleasant and accommodate), and is called (according to the name of its first founder) Harvard Colledge."

— from *New England's First Fruits*, 1643

The Overseers of the College adopted this design for a seal in 1643. The actual seal of that year, of which there exists only a single impression in the Harvard University Archives, lacked text on the three open books; it has been suggested by Samuel Elliot Morrison that the engraver wasn't up to putting it there. A chevron was added to help the composition, and to keep it from looking like a strange face. President Quincy, in his *History* of *Harvard University*, 1840, reproduced the next seal, that of the Corporation of President and Fellows, 1650, but he added vertical hatchings on the field of the shield. In modern heraldry this means gules, or red; and from this came the notion that crimson had been the Harvard color since 1650. The style of the 1650 seal was used for the first Harvard bookplates, engraved by Nathaniel Hurd in 1765. The page opposite is from this.

CONNECTICUT

Forty noblemen, knights and gentlemen incorporated in 1620 under King James I's patent as "the council established at Plymouth in the county of Devon, for the planting, ruling and governing of New-England in America." In 1628 the Plymouth company granted to Sir Henry Roswell, Sir John Young, knights, and Messrs Southcoat, Humphrey, Endicott and Witcomb, that part of New-England between the Merrimack and Charles rivers "in the bottom of Massachusetts Bay," and three miles north and south, "from the Atlantic sea and ocean on the east part, to the south sea (the Pacific Ocean) on the west part." In 1631, the earl of Warwick, president of the council of New-England, granted to Viscount Say and Seal, and to Robert Lord Brook, Sir Richard Saltonstall and others, that part of New-England called Narraganset river, 40 leagues along the seashore. The earl of Warwick had received this tract the year before from the council of Plymouth, and he received a patent for it from King Charles I. This is the original patent of Connecticut.

Sir Richard Saltonstall brought a number of emigrants over from England; they first settled at Watertown and then went to Weathersfield, in Connecticut, and were the first English settlers there. These settlers came under the patent of Viscount Say and Seal, Lord Brook and their associates.

In 1631, Wahquimacut, a chief on the Connecticut river, went to Plymouth and Boston and asked the governors there to send settlers to his river, the *Quonehtacut*, or long river. The chief promised to supply the newcomers with corn, and he told how fruitful the country there was. Governor Winslow of Plymouth soon went off to look over Connecticut.

The Indian visitor wanted English settlements in his neighborhood because Pekoath, chief of the Pequots, was busy conquering his territory.

Governor Winslow and Mr. Bradford proposed to Governor Winthrop in Boston, that they all join together and build a trading house on the Connecticut river, to barter for hemp and beaver, and to keep the Dutch out. The Boston men were not interested, for a sand bar kept larger ships from coming into the river, and there were too many warlike natives nearby. The Plymouth people decided to make a settlement there on their own.

But the Dutch got a hold on the river first, and when Mr. Holmes and the Plymouthmen arrived at the river, they found a Dutch fort already built, with cannon where Hartford now stands. The Dutch offered to shoot Holmes if he entered the river, but Holmes entered anyway, set up a house, and fortified it, at what is now Windsor. Governor van Twiller at New Amsterdam sent seventy men to drive out Holmes and the Plymouth men.

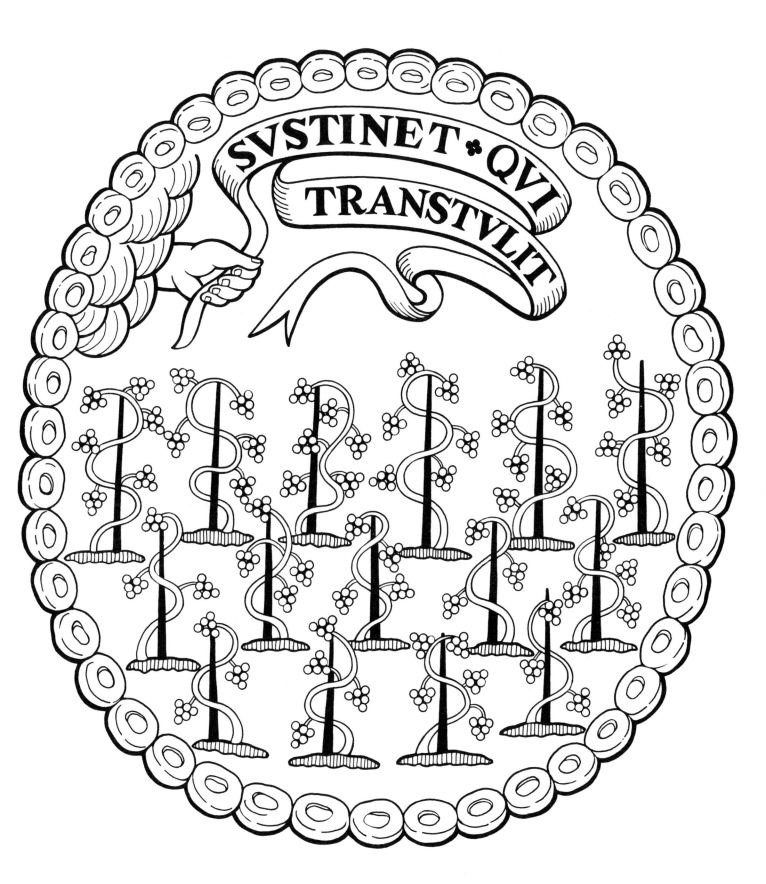

Connecticut

The Dutch marched up with flags flying to Holmes' little fort, but found it too strong to drive out the occupants. The Connecticut river was worth quarreling over because it was an easy route to the lakes and to the Indians of Canada, and thousands of valuable beaver and other pelts would be brought down it.

In 1635, sixty men, women and children with horses and cattle and pigs journeyed from Massachusetts through the wilderness to the Connecticut River. John Winthrop then went with fifty men to the mouth of the river, where he built a good fort, with cannon. A Dutch ship soon appeared to take the river, but the English prevented this. Mr. Winthrop was appointed governor of the Connecticut River. Three towns were then settled there: Windsor, at first called Dorchester; Hartford, at first called Newtown; and Weatherfield, at first called Watertown. Another colony was projected for Quinnipiack, afterwards called New-Haven. In 1637 people went there from Boston with the Reverend Mr. Davenport, a famous minister. Land was obtained from Momauguin in return for articles and protection he had already received from the English against the fierce Pequots. The New-Haven adventurers were the most wealthy company to come to New England. They set out to build an elegant city.

In 1639, the planters on the Connecticut river met at Hartford and adopted a "free and happy" constitution of their own, with a bill of rights, as they were living outside of the Massachusetts patent. Mr. George Fenwick and two ships full of emigrants arrived at Quinnipiack. Mr. Fenwick was Agent for the Proprietors of Connecticut under the earl of Warwick's patent, and he was there to plant the city at the mouth of the river. This was named Saybrook after Lord Say and Seal, and Lord Brook.

It was said in 1759 by Roger Wolcott, sometime governor of Connecticut, that Mr. Fenwick gave Connecticut the colony's seal, probably in 1644, when the old Fort Saybrook was purchased. The earliest existing impression of the seal dates from 1647. This seal was used until 1687, when Sir Edmund Andros took over the government. The vines on it represent the new colony brought over and planted in the wilderness. We read in the 80th Psalm: "Thou has brought a vine out of Egypt. Thou hast cast out the heathen and planted it." The motto states in Latin that He who brought over (the vine) continues to take care of it.

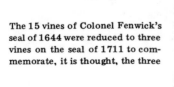

The 15 vines of Colonel Fenwick's seal of 1644 were reduced to three vines on the seal of 1711 to commemorate, it is thought, the three colonies of Saybrook, New Haven and Hartford. These three colonies were united in 1644 and 1662.

Love of Country Triumphed, 1732, from a Bill issued by the New London Society United for Trade and Commerce

AMOR PATRIA VICIT

Connecticut

NEW YORK CITY

In 1664, King Charles II granted to "our deare Brother" James, Duke of York, "all the land from the west side of Connectecutte River to the East side of De la Ware Bay," and Long Island, Martha's Vineyard, and some of Maine. The Dutch were in New Netherland, but they and grantees in Massachusetts, Connecticut and Maine were disregarded. The Duke of York, who was Lord High Admiral, sent four warships under Colonel Richard Nicolls to take New Netherland. These anchored at Nyack Bay later that year, and demanded the Dutch surrender.

Peter Stuyvesant had little gun powder on hand, and little grain, so a surrender was arranged "to improve the good of the Inhabitants." Col. Nicolls became governor, and the inhabitants were "not to call this place otherwise than New York." In 1669 the city received its first English seal, for "use of upon all Publiq Concernments." The design of that seal is not known; the next seal is from 1686. On the shield on this are a windmill's sails, probably from the arms of the prosperous Burgomaster Van Cortlandt. Between the sails are beaver and flour barrels. The supporters are a sailor, with a cross-staff (used for navigation) and a lead-line (for sounding the deep), and an Indian, with a headdress of feathers. On a ribbon it states, *Sigill: Civitat: Novi: Eborace.* York, an ancient river city in England, took its name from *ure* (water) and *ac* (place), or *Euor-ac*, which became with a little change and a Latin ending, *Eboracum.*

The windmill ground flour, which was sold in barrels. Flour was by this time the main product of the city. The seal of 1686 had as a crest the Duke of York's coronet (although the year before the duke had become King James II); this was changed afterwards on a seal with the crown, as shown here.

The wax seals of the New York Colonial Manuscripts melted in a fire in 1911 so we do not know the exact date of the change.

CAROLINA

In 1629 Charles I granted to Sir Robert Heath, his attorney general, the territory between 31° and 36° latitude. Heath and his heirs and assigns were to be absolute Lords and Proprietors of the Province, to be called *Carolana*. But settlement did not begin until about 1659, when some planters went there from Virginia. The Civil War had been going on in England; King Charles I lost his head, but his son was brought back from exile in 1660, and became King Charles II. In the 17th year of his reign, 1665, the fifth of his Restoration, he made a new grant of this same territory, "from the north end of Luke Island, which lieth in the Southern Virginia seas . . . to the river of Matthias, which bordereth upon the coast of Florida." Unlike New England, Virginia had been loyal to the crown during the troubled times, and so was called the Old Dominion. Sir William Berkeley, governor of Virginia and loyal to the king, now asked the latter for the grant of Carolina (which it was now to be called) for his brother, Lord Berkeley. The grant was made to the Berkeley brothers and to six other of the king's great friends. They were Edward Hyde, earl of Clarendon, the king's great minister, whose daughter married the king's brother; George Monk, duke of Albemarle; he took the army over to the king at the end of the Civil War; Lord Craven, who lent the king money; Ashley Cooper, later earl of Shaftesbury; he led Parliament in favor of the king; Sir George Carteret, a very great navy man; Sir John Colleton; he spent large sums of money for the king. These eight men were the absolute Lords Proprietors of Carolina, and could make laws there, etc. They formed a joint-stock company for transporting colonists, and they had the Privy Council annul the earlier grant to Sir Robert Heath. In 1665 they received a second grant extending Carolina to 36° 30'.

A group of Barbadoes adventurers under Henry Vassall alighted at Cape Fear in 1664, and settled there; the town was called Charlestown. But the adventurers soon decided that a settlement further south would be better, so the Proprietors entered into an agreement with Major Yeaman for that purpose. The major was knighted and made governor of the southern part of Carolina; a fort and settlement were made at Albemarle and old Charlestown was deserted. In 1670 the Proprietors sent Captain Sayle to settle at Port Royal. A year later, the settlers moved to the west bank of the Ashley River, and began a new Charleston. Capt. Sayle died and Yeamans became governor. The present Charleston was established in 1679 at Oyster Point where the Ashley and Cooper rivers meet.

The Proprietors' acts were authenticated by their great seal, which was kept in London and can still be seen there at the Public Records Office. Shown here is the obverse side of the seal, two crossed cornucopias, symbols of plenty, on a shield, with Indian supporters, and a stag, from the arms of

Carolina, 1665

Carolina, 1665
reverse

Carteret, as a crest about a helmet. The motto *Domitus Cultoribus Orbis*, means ... "Ruled by the cultivators of the earth." No contemporary description of this seal exists, so you may color it as you please. The reverse of the seal had all of the eight Proprietors' arms around in a circle.

The Proprietors changed over the years through inheritance and sale. The Proprietary government was weak and unable to protect the settlers from Indians and pirates (see Bellerophon's GREAT PIRATES). So, in 1715, Lord Carteret sadly wrote, "We, the Proprietors of Carolina, are utterly unable to afford our colony suitable assistance." The Lords Commissioners of Trade and Plantations said that if the nation had to go to the expense of protecting the distressed Carolinians, the crown ought to possess the government there. The crown purchased seven-eighths of the Carolinas in 1729, and Lord Carteret's one-eighth was transfered a little later.

MAINE

THE ANCHOR AND CODFISH SEAL

1661 and 1753

Maine, in 1661, began to be recognized as a part of the Province of Massachusetts Bay. Plymouth had, by the Kennebec Patent to William Bradford, nearly all the land in Maine of any value at that time. Plymouth sold its land there in 1661 to Edward Tyng, Antipas Boyes, Thomas Brattle and John Winslow. The new owners took the anchor and codfish for their emblem, along with the motto: NEC FRUSTRA DEDIT REX — the king did not give it in vain.

The Plymouth Company had about thirty members, some of the most important men of the Province of Massachusetts Bay. In 1753 they voted to have a common seal, to be made by Thomas Johnson, the eminent engraver of Boston. They now used the anchor and codfish emblem and the motto of 1661.

From the beginning the codfish had been an important emblem in New England. When America was discovered, most of Europe and England were Catholic, and fish was eaten much of the time. The codfisheries provided rich harvests and became the major industry of New England. In the old State House in Boston, which burned down in 1749, a codfish hung in the legislation hall. The codfish also appeared on bills of credit and on court seals. An Indian chief of the Seneca once declared that the codfish was truly the emblem of justice, since it bore scales.

From the actual seal, made by Thomas Johnson, now in the Massachusetts Historical Society

Maine

NEW JERSEY

Seal of New Albion
obverse

Seal of New Albion,
reverse

In 1632 an Irishman, Sir Edmund Plowden, asked King Charles I for Long Island and thirty square miles "on the adjoining continent" to be called New Albany in what was later West Jersey. Plowden and his associates agreed to settle 500 inhabitants there, and so they received the royal patent of the grant. In 1634 Sir Edmund's three sons took over. The elder, Edmund Plowden, became Lord Proprietor and Earl Palatine and Governor and Captain General of the hopeful Company of New Albion. In 1643, he was marooned by his ship's crew on Smith's Island. An English ship rescued him and took him to the Delaware Bay. There, with the help of Governor Prinz of New Sweden, he recovered his stolen barque. He returned to England and in 1648 he proposed the chivalrous Order of the Albion Knights, with this seal. His coroneted person was on one side. On the other were the arms of New Albion, dexter, and his own arms, sinister. An open Gospel surmounted by a hand dexter issued from the parti line grasping a sword erect, surmounted by a crown. The Plowden arms are a fesse dancettée (an indented belt, one-third of the field) with two fleurs de lis on the upper points. The supporters were two bucks rampant gorged (collared) with crowns, the whole surmounted by the coronet of the Earl Palatine, and surrounded with the motto: *Sic Suos Virtus Beat*. (Thus does Virtue bless her followers). Settlers, though, were not attracted by notions of chivalry, and they did not come. Sir Edmund died in 1659, and the Plowden claim became hazy.

The settlement of New Sweden began in the Delaware valley, at Murderkill Creek, in 1638. It was begun by Willem Usselinx, a founder of the Dutch West India Company, who had a falling out with his patrons over his salary and so offered to work for the great king of Sweden, Gustavus Adolphus. Peter Minuit, whom you remember from Manhattan Island in New Netherland, also became unhappy with his employers. It was Minuit who established Fort Christina in New Sweden; then he sailed to the West Indies, where he was lost in a storm. Governor John Prinz led the fourth Swedish expedition to the Delaware in 1643. The seal of New Sweden was to be his personal seal, "until times improved," which they didn't. In 1651 Peter Stuyvesant marched over New Jersey with a small army, and took over the Delaware River. And in 1655 Stuyvesant came with a small fleet, and made Captain Schulte of New Sweden surrender. Nine years later, Stuyvesant's New Netherland, in turn, became New York.

King Charles II and his brother the duke of York had friends who had helped them during the years of the Civil War. Lord John Berkeley and Sir George Carteret — two of the Proprietors of Carolina — were such friends. The duke of York granted them, as true and absolute Lords Proprietors, all of the province from the Hudson River to Cape May to the Delaware Bay and River

After an impression of the Great Seal of the Proprietors, 1665, showing calipers, scales, corn and wheat, symbols of fair division and productivity

East Jersey

to the Hudson River, to be called New Caesarea or New Jersey — in honor of Carteret's defence of the Isle of Jersey in 1649 when attacked by Cromwell's forces. Here is an illustration of the Great Seal of the Proprietors of New Caesarea or New Jersey, of which there now exists only a single impression. The arms of Berkeley are in duplicate with those of Carteret. In 1664 Berkeley and Carteret drew up "The Concessions and agreements of the Lords Proprietors of the Province of New Caesarea or New Jersey to and with all and every the Adventurers and all such as shall settle or plant there." This was called the Magna Carta of New Jersey. It granted rights, which included freedom of worship. Besides these rights, every freeman who came with a good musket was promised 150 acres of land.

But in 1673 the Dutch sent a squadron with 600 soldiers to take New York and New Jersey. The following year, however, by a treaty the territory went back to the English. That year Governor Andros came over to rule in autocratic fashion and to annul the Jersey grants. At this time too, Major Fenwick with Edward Byllynge, Quakers, bought Lord Berkeley's half interest in New Jersey. Byllynge had 9/10 of the purchase. In 1676 the colonies of East and West Jersey were separated. Sir George Carteret received East Jersey and William Penn and his associates received West Jersey. Associations of Quakers in Yorkshire and in London in England were established to colonize West Jersey. The "Concession and Agreements of the Proprietors, Freeholders, and Inhabitants of West New Jersey in America" established the spirit of democracy there and religious freedom. Settlers soon began to arrive in large numbers: 250 came on the ship *Kent* in 1677. The duke of York made another grant of West Jersey to William Penn and his friends in 1680, and the Fenwick part was soon obtained by Penn's group too.

In East Jersey Governor Carteret struggled with Governor Andros of New York over the authority of the province. Andros had Carteret arrested. But the duke of York, for whose authority Andros acted, soon granted all of the duke's interest in East Jersey to the then Sir George Carteret. The duke wrote that Andros had had no authority over East Jersey, so the obnoxious Andros went home to England. He would return soon enough.

Sir George Carteret died and Lady Elizabeth Carteret took over the administration of East Jersey. William Penn and eleven of his associates purchased the territory from her in 1681. In 1702 Queen Anne accepted the surrender of the right of government by the proprietor of East and West Jersey, and that was the end of the use of the seals which are illustrated here. Alas, the queen sent a very bad royal governor, one Edward Hyde, Lord Cornbury. The New Jersey Assembly in time protested, and he was removed in 1708. A spirit of resistance had begun.

West Jersey

PENNSYLVANIA

William Penn was born October 14, 1644. His father was a great naval hero. His mother was Dutch, and had "more wit than her husband," according to Pepys. Young Penn grew up during a period of civil war and religious chaos, during these days George Fox founded the Religious Society of Friends. William became interested in this new doctrine while he was a student at Oxford and was fined for taking part in it. This dismayed his father the admiral, who tried to alter his son's ways — to no avail. So William was sent to the continent, where he met Algernon Sydney (you will read about him when you come to the Sword-In-Hand seal.) Then William was called home to serve with his father, now captain commander of the duke of York's great fleet against the Dutch.

But William became very serious and spent his time reading. His father then sent him to Ireland, to live in the family castle. There he went to hear his old Quaker teacher from Oxford. William was arrested and put in jail with all the other listeners. Admiral Penn had his son released, called him to London, and then threw him out of the house. In London, William saw George Fox more and more. Soon young Penn wrote a little book called *Truth Exalted*, which was about "the life and doctrine of the despised Quakers as the alone good old way of life and salvation." It was signed "William Penn . . . not fearing the king's wrath." He then wrote a pamphlet called "The Guide Mistaken" and was locked up in the Tower of London for it. "I owe my conscience to no mortal man," said William from jail; "tell the king," he said, "that power is the worst argument in the world."

After many months the king finally let him out. William, finding the Quaker meeting house locked, began preaching outside — and was again arrested, and now put in Newgate Prison. He was tried at the Old Bailey, and was acquitted. The judge was furious at the acquittal, and imposed heavy fines on each of the jurors as well as on Penn. Then William wrote *The Great Cause of Liberty of Conscience.* After his release he went to Holland, where he heard all about America. In 1672 he married a Quaker, Gulielma Springett.

Lord Berkeley and Sir George Carteret owned New Jersey. Lord Berkeley became disenchanted with it, and, since there were already some Friends there, he wished to sell his part to George Fox, who had just returned from America. Berkeley sold his interest for a thousand pounds to John Fenwick for Edward Byllynge, Friends both. But Byllynge, becoming pecuniarily embarrassed (broke), transferred his interest to Penn and his associates. The province was divided, and Penn's part was West Jersey. Many Friends came, and the province prospered.

The government owed his father 16,000 pounds, but the exchequer was empty, so Penn thought, why not accept a province in America for the debt?

From an impression of the Great Seal of William Penn, 3 inches in diameter, obverse; Pennsylvania Historical and Museum Commission

Pennsylvania

He received a charter from King Charles on March 4, 1681 for what Penn first proposed calling "New Wales" and then "Sylvania" (Woodland) since forest covered most of the land. But the king added *Penn* as a prefix, in honor of the admiral. William thought this a great piece of vanity, and offered money to have it changed. "Had he bribed the king, he might have had his wish," it was said. The territory was from the Delaware River to 43° north latitude, westward 5°, southerly to a circle twelve miles north of Newcastle, then to 40° latitude, then westward to the beginning. The payment to the crown was to be two beaver skins delivered at Windsor Castle every January first. This was paid every year until near the end of the American Revolution. In 1682, Penn purchased more territory on the Delaware River from the duke of York; this was later known as the Lower Counties: New Castle, Kent and Sussex.

Penn sent his cousin, Colonel Markham, to take possession of the country for the new Proprietor and Governor. He sent a letter along to the settlers there in which he said, "you shall be governed by laws of your own making, and live a free, and if you will, a sober and industrious people." The ships *John and Sarah*, the *Bristol Factor*, and the *Welcome* brought many new settlers who landed at the Swedish settlements on the Delaware River. Penn wrote instructions for the founding of a town. Each house was to "pitch upon the middle of the plot" so that there would be gardens all around, and it would be "a green country town, which will never be burnt and always wholesome." He also said that the settlers should obtain the "love and concent" of the Indians. "I went thither to lay the foundation of a free colony for all mankind," wrote Penn.

Penn looked for a place for the provincial capital, and found the best spot on a neck of land where the Delaware and Schulykill rivers meet. The land was bought from three Swedish brothers, the Svensons. Here, on twelve miles square, Penn laid out Philadelphia. The first structure built was the *Blue Anchor* tavern, but in a few months the town counted eighty houses and within two years, there were 500. The new Assembly passed Penn's Great Law, which included a section requiring every child twelve years old to begin to learn a trade or skill.

The Penn arms became the arms of the province, and the Penn seal became the seal of the Colony. The earliest Great Seal of Pennsylvania was enormous, three inches or more in diameter. The Penn arms were a silver (argent) shield, crossed horizontally by a black (sable) fess or band, bearing on it three silver torteux or bisquits, with the motto *Mercy, Justice*. The counterseal or reverse shows three radiating ears of Indian corn and three grape vines (Penn was quite interested in growing grapes and making wine to attract Frenchmen), surrounded by a band bearing the words *Truth, Peace, Love* and *Plenty*, and the whole was surrounded by an olive branch.

Pennsylvania

COLONY OF GEORGIA

In 1717, Sir Robert Montgomery secured a grant from the Lords Proprietors of Carolina of all lands lying between the Alatamaha and Savannah Rivers. Sir Robert wrote glowingly about his *New Colony* to the South of Carolina in *the most delightful Country of the Universe,* but then nobody came to settle there. In 1720, King George I feared that either the French or the Spanish would occupy the Alatamaha River, so the Governor of South Carolina was sent there to take it as part of his colony. Then, in 1730, 7/8 of Carolina was sold by the Lords Proprietors to the Crown for 22,500 pounds; Lord Carteret kept his 1/8th part, but in 1732 he conveyed that for the establishment of the colony of Georgia.

James Oglethorpe was in the House of Commons, interesting himself in the relief of unfortunate debtors who, in those days, were put into prison. It occurred to him that these souls might immigrate to the territory between the above-mentioned rivers. Good Mr. Oglethorpe would himself gain nothing by these settlements. A Royal Charter was granted in 1732: the poor debtors would find honorable work there; they would provide protection against the fierce Indians on the frontiers of Carolina, and trade would increase. Oglethorpe and other important Englishmen formed the "Trustees for establishing the Colony of Georgia in America." They were granted the territory and the privilege of transporting there as many subjects as should be willing to go. Lord Viscount Percival was named the first president of the corporation. This seal was the colony's first seal, and it was used from 1732 to 1733. Fraudulent use of it soon necessitated another seal, which was rather similar. The two river gods, with seaweed in their hair, hold urns from which flow the rivers on the northern and southern boundaries of the colony, the Altamaha and the Savannah. In their other hands appear a tobacco leaf and a bottle. Georgia sits majestically between them holding a spear which represents protection and a cornucopia which represents plenty. The inscription, *Colonia Georgia Aug(eat),* means "May the Colony of Georgia Grow." The reverse side of the seal shows a silkworm on a mulberry leaf; such plants grew in Georgia, and it was hoped that the silk industry could become established there. The inscription on the reverse, *Non Sibi sed Aliis,* means "Not for ourselves but for others." It refers to the selfless manner in which the silkworms spun for others as well as to Oglethorpe's generosity.

Georgia

THE NEW ENGLAND PINE TREE

A "green tree" was the early emblem of Massachusetts, but it soon came to be known as a pine-tree. The famous "pine-tree" shilling was minted in Massachusetts in 1652. It is shown here greatly enlarged. The inscription, *MASATHUSETS IN* continues on the other side, *NEW ENGLAND, 1652, XII* (for 12 pence). The tree was used on flags of New England, but it "no more resembles a pine-tree than a cabbage," it was said — and that could apply to the shilling, too. The following story, passed on by Preble, suggests that it may have been another kind of tree.

> When Charles II learned the colonies' assumption of one of his prerogatives to coin money, he was very angry; his wrath was, however, appeased by Sir Charles Temple, a friend of the colony, who told him they thought it no crime to coin money for their own use; and, taking some of the money from his pocket, handed it to the king, who asked him what tree that was upon it. "That," replied Sir Charles, "is the royal oak which preserved your Majesty's life." His remark put the king in a good humor, and he heard what Sir Charles had to say in their favor, calling them "a parcel of honest dogs."

The young king had hidden in a tree during the Civil War.

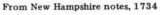

From New Hampshire notes, 1734

A Great Struggle

Bellerophon Books have several exciting works about the American Revolution which you will enjoy. Peruse the list opposite, and let us send you a catalog.